# R.ℜ.P.

Trapp Family Publishing LLC
*The $45,000 Cat and Other Poems*

Copyright Ⓒ 2016: David W. Trapp

ISBN: 978-0-9800946-8-8
ISBN: 0-9800946-8-2

This book, additional titles, stuffed toy animals, and accessories based on *Daxton and Miranda Adventure Books* can be found at:

# MYINJUREDPET.COM

## Other Books Written by
*David W Trapp:*

A Conservative Terrorist:
*The Demise of Walter Reed*

Plates of Gold and Other Spiritual Poems

The Donkey and the Elephant

"Miraculous Majesty Flies Again"
*A Daxton and Miranda Adventure*

"Tipsy Russell Recovers"
*A Daxton and Miranda Adventure*

"Army Dill Gets Shelled"
*A Daxton and Miranda Adventure*

"Kitty Gets Leveled"
*A Daxton and Miranda Adventure*

"Tom Turkey Gets Pardoned"
*A Daxton and Miranda Adventure*

"Rudolph Misses the Roof"
*A Daxton and Miranda Adventure*

# The $45,000 Cat
*And Other Poems*


Written By:


# David W. Trapp

*Every author (or poet) should have at least one book dedicated to his parents, and this the one for me. My parents did a fine job in raising twelve children (one died) and it is definitely not their fault that one of their sons writes poetry. Of course, the old saying goes; "the apple don't fall far from the tree". Makes you wonder whose influence it was that brought all these poems out,,,,was it Mom? Or was it Dad? I personally think they both ought to own up to their responsibility, and take 50/50 blame (or credit) as the case may be!*

# $45,000 Cat

Money for a dog-killed cat
Makes me say "what's up with that?"
We abort children e'er more
Though murdered cats we abhor
Cat gets chomped by mean doggy
Leaving carcass torn and soggy
Owner cries now filled with dread
Seeing that his cat is dead
Sues his neighbor, former friend
Whose dog saw to kitty's end
He wins a lotto, shouts with glee
Thank you, thank you, dead kitty
It's a shame we show more care
For cats, not kids, lives we dare
To throw away, total waste
Away this life with such haste
This our more society
Is not with, I wish to be

## Murder

Abortion is not an option for me
Why would I murder a tiny baby
That child has a soul and is alive
Any word to the opposite is only jive
When women say it's my body my choice
They are not thinking of baby's right to rejoice
Instead act selfish, they want no responsibility
They would rather not add to the family tree
Crying, moaning belittling their act
It's still a baby, and that's a fact.

# My snack

Cheese and apples
Apples and cheese
To my taste buds
Saying thank you and please
Cut off the skins
Wedges wrapped with slices
Take a bite of both
My taste bud it entices
I finish the snack
My tray is now clean
Eating cheese and apples
Strengthens my spleen.

## Lies

Uptown girls with downtown guys
Both look up seeking the skies
Searching for truth in each others eyes
Truth is susceptible as are lies.

## Not me

Who wants to be known as a poet of death?
Emily, Walt, John or Seth – not me
I would rather be revered with bright tomes
By the people who work to build up their homes.

## Expressive

Wind ruffling hair so brown
Shielding her face
I look for her eyes
Expressive
We walk the beach
Hold hands and talk
Beautiful grey skies
Expressive
Hugging her close
Feeling her warmth
Comfort her cries
Expressive
Loving her walk
Wanting her close
We search the skies
Expressive
With love I look
Upon this lady
My heart with her lies
Expressive.

## Sharks

Whenever we wake wide-eyed wondering
Remembering recent recurring remarks
Anger abounding answers anyone
Should shunning shining or shelving shrewd sharks?

## Guthrie

Oppressive teachers of English they say
Do not listen to students – not their way
Their standards are capricious, arbitrary
Taking English classes you need be wary

## Miss Nomer

I met someone nice the other day
Really had nothing important to say
So to this person I gave a big hug
Love I told her was the ultimate drug
Write a rhyming verse I said to her
Someone will read it that's a big for sure
So she tried and tried and once more for luck
With her tongue in her cheek she said I'm stuck
I can't write the words for others to see
A great poet she laments I'll never be
Telling her remember Emily now
In her tower, never throwing in the towel
Gazing out her window on New England
Her paper on the sill her pen in her hand
Thoughts in her head it's all she wrote
Reading her crap asks for a quick garrote
If she can, you can its all I do say
Take up your pen and write now today
Give me your words your dreams and your ideal
Until, like Emily, in your solace we steal
Away from you we go up and down slopes
Your dreams words we share thoughts and hopes.

# Time Stops

Today time is stopping
Neither forward nor back
Class is really hopping
Wanting to stay on track

The clock is still ticking
But not keeping good time
Minute hand keeps sticking
With no reason or rhyme

The class however is talking
Not keeping up with the clock
Like birds the students are flocking
For their education they end up in hock.


## RST262

A monk holding a begging bowl and staff
Wearing a basket hat that makes me laff
I hand him coins and bow to him deeply
A way of getting blessed quite cheaply.

## Blind

An ostrich stuck his head in a hole
Wondering which way his enemies go
Thinking he is safe and sound
The truth was different than what he found

Hearing no noise he pulled out his head
Looking around he sees his friends dead
What have I done is what he wonders
Right or wrong are ideas he ponders

No more sticking my head in the sand
I'll be the bravest ostrich in the land
Contemplate, act, don't stand around
I made a mistake – put my head in the ground.

## Roads

The road of life will not show you
You can travel the road of life or not
Even when you do not travel you do
A life lever that did not get switched
That will lead you to an end you ditched
Wondering why you ended up there
When you reach that end will you truly care?
You say you won't, it affects you not
But life is funny though it ends up in a plot
Does it end there or does the road go on?

## Ticking

When time ticks tocking
Hears my heart hocking
Wend wayward walking
Till thy words talking
Many men mocking
Women wildly willing
Children, chicks chilling
Deep depths docking
People penning prose
Gradient garbage grows
Towards troubling towers
Shines shining showers
Finished it finally is
Wearily we wake
Floating like a flake
She knows it's his.

## Military Might

The water laps at the side of the ship
While through the water we silently slip
Heading to our destination unknown
To other countries our power we loan
We feel as if they want us around here
They play into their just and unjust fear
If through their lands we do freely roam
When in truth we should be closer to home
That question I ask with impunity
Can they (and I) be blind to what we see?

# Direction

Simply slightly sickly says she
Mashing meds makes mom most mopey
Finding forgotten fun flitting
Love loves lovers long life lifting
When wives weep with welling wisdom
Fighting feelings forming freedom
Knowing nuptials nothing new needs
Protected person part pleased
Grayer gradient growing
Hearing heavenly hoeing
Determining direction done
Wedded winsome winner won
Needed nothing no one never
People provide post palaver
Drove drugged demented drooling
Tested Trapp tall talked tooling.

## Puddles

If I watched the rain
Or felt it on my face
Would I be any happier
Living in the rat race
Or would I still believe
That all I do and say
Does not mean a thing
I still have debts to pay
So there I stand in the rain
It is puddling at my feet
Worrying about my future
While standing in the street.

# Mirrors

He looked in the mirror and what did he see
A gray haired old man looking back at me
On his face was a look of great surprise
He had gotten old right before his eyes.

He looked in the mirror and what did he see
A middle-aged guy looking out at me
He wondered why he was where he was
His choices had led him there just because.

He looked in the mirror and what did he see
A young guy with lots of potential maybe
He thought he would be famous and rich
Hold to the rod and stay out of the ditch.

He could have been someone so he thought
If into the truth he had bought
It wasn't really so, but it seemed to be
What he wanted most was to add to the tree.

# Usurper

Unable to attend
His duke he did send
To stand in with his word
In deference to his lord
With sword offered
On bended knee
Peace he proffered
Life's prosperity
Accepted is the sword
With a nod Duke did rise
In his robe a hidden cord
It's just the right size
Slipped around the neck
Of the upstart king
Thinking what the heck
I'll steal his ring
Usurper of power
Sword Duke does wield
Commands the tower
 Quieting bells pealed
The alarm has sounded
It was heard with chagrin
His Lord was bounded
To send his men in
The castle they storm
A furious fight
Quashing the worm
To make it all right
The lord in the end
Is the winner by far
He no longer has to tend
Duke's head in the jar.

# Poems

Expressing myself with kind words
Is exhilarating to me
I can write beautiful pictures
For the whole world to enjoy, see

I practice my art every chance
With pen I jot all my word thoughts
With a vast room for improvement
Perfection is what I have sought

If, with my writings I can help
People, by reading my soft words
They are directed for persons
Those who find it unbind cords.

## Blood

My life slowly trickles
Through the blood in my hands
Beating out through the wound that I have.
As I look slowly up at my killer
He laughs aloud in my face
Little does he know that I
Am the one who won the race.
You see, I may be dying
But he still has to live
With the knowledge of my death
That I will or will not forgive
So I smile up at his face
He has a bewildered gaze
Wondering why I smile
As I embrace death's daze.

# Time

To those people of the earth
Who have never watched a star fall
From the sky so dark and clear
To the ground so dense and near
For those people who smell
City sewers each and every day
But do not smell the roses
By the window sill
Who only care about
The money in the till
To those people who waste
Their lives are just numbers
Never stopping to hug family
Knowing not but heavy seas
Give those people a hand
Hold thoughts for them to have
Stop, slow down, enjoy
Take your time
Down to earth
Oh boy.

# Windy

Here I sit with the wind at my back
Its leaves are gently tickling my neck
While whistling away at a tune aimlessly
It must be the south wind famously
This wind continues to press relentlessly
On my body as if to push me down the hill
Atop of which I view my domain
I gather my limbs into the fold
Still the wind tries to destroy me
Pushing with all its will but I know
That it will be forever and a day
Before that wind takes my breath away.

# Yesteryear

I tripped alongside a sparkling brook
During my yesteryears gone by
I listened to the sounds it made
Laughing, gurgling, I heard its sigh
While I studied the stream so clear
I realized that it had life
Its mission was to provide enjoyment
While easing person's inner strife
I let this brook's spirit flow
Over my body filling me with peace
A joyful feeling fills my breast
One I wished would never cease
I still recall that brook at times
Whenever despair fills my heart
Memories of it lighten my day
With feelings I'll never depart

## Wrote

I wrote this book
To let others see
The happiness I have
Inside of me
If you buy this book
You will find out
What happiness is
Is all about!

## Times

I remember times
Together we share
Happiness in each
Sharing love and care.
Those were fun fun days
Happiness our goal
Reality struck
Taking heavy toll.
Now we are parted
Never times forget
Keeping memories
Each in other's debt.

# Trek

Rain came pelting down
Hard on my bare back
I just kept walking
along that swampy track.

Soon I am sloshing
Through mud to my neck
Yet I keep plodding
On my lonesome trek.

Every twist and turn
Greater things I see
Even though I'm tired
Strong is what I'll be.

I now reach my goal
My dreary trudging
Mud, water and sand
The way was grudging.

Up, forward onward
The top I must go
Using talent, brains
Never the word NO!

## Windy Love

Like birds soaring
Or trees rustling
On the wind
Our love is buffeted
Weakly objecting
Pushed up, dropped down
With a shudder
We come within a hair
Of losing our love
Forever.
Somehow it always
Climbs so high
On the updraft
Of our emotions
This, our love
Conveyed to the other
During quiet lulls
Always knowing
Our love is shared
Forever.

# Cruisin

With the waters lapping
On the side of the ship
The Captain is mapping
Our route for the trip

Ready are the sailors
As they stand by the rail
No need for the bailers
Our backup is a sail

The ship is underway
Across the Atlantic
Our wives trust what we say
So they are not frantic

Fourteen days of rocking
We finally spot land
At the dock we're docking
Workers give us a hand

The Medit we did reach
From the start twas our goal
Now five months on the beach
Call it Navy Patrol

Months later we head back
Missing loved ones in mind
Captain has a certain knack
Our homeland he will find.

## Separated

While sitting here
Sipping my pop
'membering you
I'll never stop
Music I listen
Daydream the while
Separated
Mile upon mile
I think how nice
See you once more
Beautiful lady
Whom I adore
You know my thoughts
Dreams you know too
I've shared them all
Only with you.


## Day Dreaming

How many times do I watch the clouds drifting
Lazing about through thoughts my mind sifting
Every time I daydream about times shared
With you, the times for each other we cared
That's how I always end up the day crying
It could have been but now I am dying
Why did you go where have you gone
I'm tortured, you been gone so long
Will you return sending me a sign
For you forever I will toe the line.

## Always

High on the hillside green
Where the grass gently sways
It's more beautiful, it seems
In the sun's bright rays
We walk hand in hand
To the mountaintop
Our love binds us together
And it will never stop
Together we are
Always we will be
The words "I love you"
Mean so much to me.

## Broke Again

When things get rough
I'm out of dough
I use Visa
Need things to go
I have plenty
Lots of money
Twenty-five smacks
Can't buy honey
I'm still happy
Still I am broke
If anyone laughs
Give them a poke.

# Bells for the Wed

Listening to the music
Playing tunes in my head
Joyous ringing, clearly
Bells for the wed.

She in her soft white gown
Standing sweetly there
As she awaits him now
Thinking, "do I dare"

The two of them
Wed for all time
Bells ring again
Pealing a chime

They are truly happy
As they forge ahead
In life together
Bells for the wed.

## A Wish

If I only had one wish
To do with what I wanted
My first thought is riches
I could then have flaunted
Discard my first thought
I quickly change my mind
To have a thousand gems
Valuable, every kind
Dropped that idea also
To live, yes forever
Be very successful
My every endeavor
Like the first and second
The last I quickly forgot
Being with her
Is what I truly sought.

## Good Guys

I write a lot of poems
I read a lot of books
I watch a lot of movies
That are filled with lots of crooks.
I always root and yell
For the good guys dressed in white
They beat up all the bad guys
In every single fight
I shall write a movie
Just watch me and see
The bad guys will lose again
The good guys include me!

## Dear Children

To behold and see
Joy on small faces
Lights my own face with joy
They are so cheerful
Those little children
To hold them and listen
They have their problems too
Fears and doubts assail them
We who are older
Should respect those feelings
From those children
Help them grow taller
Become strong in all things
Help them to become adults
Without the usual strings.

# Hello There World

Hello there world
So innocent
And so naïve
You wandering
Blindly our paths
Now to conceive
Hello there world
Begin to merge
Christ has come now
Your sins to purge
Hello there world
Know and realize
Narrow the way
In Father's eyes
Hello there world
End drawing near
You've been righteous
Nothing to fear.

## Our Bodies

Life's blood is flowing
Through my veins
Listen to the pumping
Of my heart
Watching my muscles
Work every day
Stand in secret awe
The workmanship used
On the human body
Truly in God's image
We have been created
How wonderful, unique
Nothing to compare
With our bodies.

# Stars

Stars twinkling overhead
They brighten the dark
High above us traveling
While time they do mark.

Slowly they wink out
Another night passes
We lie there wayward
In the morning grasses.

They are still up there
Forever they do stay
When they give no light
Know that it is day.

Awaiting the next night
Watch again for stars
Can we capture them
In our small clear jars.

Then we hold them tight
Forever they're close by
We could have a night
In the daytime sky.

Oh beautiful stars
Will you shine once more
To brighten my night
And fill it with lore.

## Sweet Music

To sit enveloped
In sweet music
Feeling it flow
Through my body
Relaxing my senses
Let's me drift
With my thoughts
Warmly encasing
My whole being
Like a cloud
Softly bearing
Sweets to a child
Music I hear
In my heart
Leaves me smiling
Sweet music.

## Traveling

My travels around this world
Has led me to many lands
I've met numerous people
Shook so many hands
South and North
To East and West
In all my travails
America is still best
No matter where I travel
No matter how long I stay
I will still find my home
In the good ole USA.

## Reaching Spain

After all these long lonesome days
Traveling in fourth gear
We have reached Spain
Lights are twinkling near.
Our excitement rises
We crowd around the rail
Looking over calm waters
Waiting for our mail.
Now we again see
Land not too far off
We shrug on our coats
Our hats we do doff.
We are so happy
Excited is our way
We anticipate liberty
At the end of day!

# Home to You Dear

I have counted so many stars
Driven lots of brand new cars
I have seen so many wars
Been on numerous tedious tours
But I'll always come home to you dear
To hold you so close and have you near
Don't be sorrowed now, wipe that tear
I've passed so many small towns
Done uppers and lots of downs
Walked for miles and miles
Met people with false smiles
But I'll always come home to you dear
To soothe your troubles calm your fear
Don't be disheartened wipe away that tear
So many people don't listen
Looking near when its far
I'll never lose you honey
Days forever will be sunny
Cause I'll always come home to you dear
Don't be sorrowed wipe away that tear
Don't be sorrowed wipe away that tear

## The Show

All decked out
In our dress greens
Manning the sail
Strength it means
Looking sharp, clean
People can see
How we men act
In the USMC
Spit and shine
Polish and glow
What we do best
Is put on a show
But it's enough
Most of the time
Being numero uno
Is not a crime!

## Visions

Draw a picture in your mind
What in life you wish to be
All good thoughts that you find
Keep inside for others to see
Your visions are what you are
Set your goals up high
No one keeps you from going far
If your visions never die
Work hard at all you do
You will find the reward quite just
People will be glad to meet you
If in you they can trust.

## Together

Nothing comes nothing
Everything between us two
Comes from sharing hearts
Our thoughts we share too
So if we ever stop
Our hearts beating as one
Mourning clouds will hover
Gone will be the sun
Let us stay together
Our lives we will share
Say I love you honey
I will say I care!

## Same

Bright sun over the mountaintops peeking
Truth in our lives we're constantly seeking
Knowing what's right in this we are trusting
From woman's warm hearts love we are wresting
We cling to our lives earn our daily due
Like pigeons pair to each other we coo
With warm kisses and hugs we show our love
Together we can climb mountains above
We believe the same way think the same too
Our love has been strong since saying I do!

## War Sonnet

Green shades of darkness filtering the sun
Shadows creeping from one to another
When the heavy sound comes help your brother
Lots more blood flowing when the day is done
Was I really here or was it a dream
Listen to silence waiting for more
The shells start falling shakes you to the core
Trickles of red meandering to stream.
Another day done horizon dimming
Trudging forward night fires smell cooking
Quiet crickets jungle noisy but not
Thinking quietly of bodies swimming
Quonset huts, warmth, food no friends be looking
Lessons learned today, at once lessons taught.

# Monster Man

Grendel, a monster eating men all night
Beowulf, a man giving monster a fright
Rothgar, a king wanting freedom right now
Beowulf, to kill monster is his proud vow
Grendel, appears now to play his last role
Beowulf, with his arm chases to a hole
Rothgar, gets his wish, Beowulf gets treasure
Mother,  of Grendel takes Beowulf's measure
Beowulf, into her lair dives water deep
Mother, fights ferociously in cave's heap
Mother's, heap is her undoing, sword wall
Beowulf, returns triumphant Rothgar's hall
Mother, and son together never 'gain
Neither, town people bother, Beowulf wins.

# Grug

At noon the invisible day and night
When darkness envelops the both of them
And we are reminded of hopelessness
Darkness completely enfolded darkness
Black night and grey days discolor the world
While certain evils are abounding there
We look to the heavens for our white light
To bright the gray and the black of night
Can it be possible colors will win
Or will the darkness be as our last sin

Weighting us down crushing inner spirits
Calling Almighty Heavenly Father
The last hope after the devil had called
Thrusting with power our lives mean nothing
We fight with every sinew now aching
Desperately we cling to our last hope
As we thrash through garbage, filth, feces, grug
Reaching the bank slippery, wet, slimey
The mud, sand, dirt crushed in our fingers
We lay exhausted breathing shallow breaths
Rolling over see the sun waking up
Its as if a whole new life is given
Do we accept the rebirth or slide back
Down the bank feeling grit, grime, hopelessness
Clutching, crying, calling, despairing yes
Knowing the cascading had to be stopped
There is no such over-exquisite peace
Casting fashion of uncertain evils
Or certain evils that we realized
Fought, conquered, persevered, overcame
Winning the struggle, the struggle is done.

# Lost

Snow cave residing in
Night falls stars shine coldest
Lost we are soon be found
Shivering cold our test
Hearing covert night sound
We are frozen apart
Though huddled together
No fuel, fire cannot start
Probably cold weather
We make it through the night
Our food is all gone now
The heavy snow traverse
Fifteen feet high to plow
No snowshoes make it worse
Words of encouragement
Whispers of love shouted
Strength each other was lent
Rescue never doubted
Shouts of joy were sounded
Over engines roaring
Hugs, each back was pounded
Feelings, thoughts were soaring
Lost two toes, one finger
Memories still linger.

## Milton

Whiling away the hour
Discussing the expected
Writing gives us power
Small brains are infected
Speaking of John Milton
Wondering will we learn
Reading marathon
Milton's hell doth burn
Hear Paradise Lost
Other poems epic
No matter the cost
Happiness doth stick
Making all the plans
Hour over almost
Class has all its clans
Giving John a toast

# The Greatest Gift

I stand at the door and knock
Will you let me in?
My arms envelop your life
There is no more sin
Today I've atoned for you
My gift accept please
Sorrow, pain, blood and despair
Never would it cease
In m y greatest hour of need
Just like yours I know
My Father in the Heavens
Presence to me shows
He is always there for me
As he is for you
Listen for me at thy door
My knocks are not few
Let me in I ask of thee
Accept me thy heart
I'm standing at thy front door
From thee never part.

# The Ride

Hold on for the ride of your life
Filled with sorrow, troubles and strife
Wild rushes, winds torrents and gusts
Torrential rains clouds billowing
Leaves and branches, tress willowing
Angry noises, rumbles and cries
Whistling through cracks, tumbling skies
No matter the weather or whether
It matters not, we are boldly
We shiver and shake not coldly
Staring with awe, wonder and fright
Wait for a sign dark skies turn light
Through the pane we see rains abate
Skies slowly clearing long await
Hugs all around, clean up the mess!

## Grim Reaper

Death never loses, not one
In the noon day sun
Or during dark dark nights
Its what gives us frights
Unless we know before
We hear the knock on the door
And then we realize
Its knocked us down to size
Sinking ever deeper
We follow the grim reaper!

## Sheri's Sonnet

My sweetheart leaves me weak-kneed
Breathless and all atwitter
Her mother tried to pit her
Against myself and our seed
Twenty four years afterward
We are together still now
To her mom we take a bow
Struck a harmonious chord

So we did not allow it
We knew we'd a perfect fit
We'd share our thoughts, hearts, minds and love
Hold tightly to each other
No looking at another
Love always my nighttime dove.

## Riddle #1

Connected but separate
Long, thin, short, pudgy and fat
Brown, black, white, yellow at that
One points way, two show date

Ten makes power, as does five
One beckons for water cold
One makes pointers oh so bold
Two together click to jive

Shortest indispensable
Middle one shows the known sign
Never shown when feeling fine
All help conquer the crucible.

## Nits

I hate getting hosed
I guess I supposed
I would go through life
With no outer strife
Strife within would be
Force affecting me
Instead what I found
What makes worlds go round
Interfering nits
Completely to bits
Find lots of trouble
Makes living double
Their life they measure
My stolen treasure

## Colours

Colours bouncing higher
They're tethered to a pole
Since sunup they are there
Informing direction
Drawing man's seeking eye
Leading the battled troops
Inspires men to die
When trampled underneath
Enraged people respond
When flying overhead
Men form a common bond
They've been there since the start
Long after we are gone
They will still be flying
Upholding liberty
Always inspiring.

# Milton's Sonnet

Form and matter, matter not
In a Milton class that's taught
Stile suited to 'nother
Though say not Milton's mother
Writing for divorce says he
Sharp double-edged libertie
Cast not your pearls before swine
Libertie licence both entwine

Owl, cuckoo, ass, ape and dogs
Jove turned two into frogs
Ensuring the Presse don't stop
Hinds never end up on top
Truth is truth and it shall be
And the truth shall make you free.

## Humph!

Hinds find me penned, very chaotic
Dogs nosing for ideas far more exotic
Unorganized they say, no grammar
Can't follow the gist, so words they hammer
I'll make it simple, as simple can be
They are similar to owls in the tree.

# Accordingly

Daily I'm alone except for my Lord
I travel and write to one accord
Though I see wrongs, I may also see rights
As I am stopping at too many lights
Intermittent motion too sporadic
Traveling from town to town, nomadic
Living life by closer observation
Never reaching my true destination
The journey is the goal, so many roads
Helping another, lightening their loads
Acting so, am I not freeing myself
Did not stack my talents on dusty shelf
Some believe my words are heavenly scent
If so, my works will never trucidant.

# Words

What beautiful rhymes fill my head
Along with the words, but no music
Thoughts, musings, randomly
Some beautiful, some not so
I have to scribble the dribble
Or go nuts instead
What beautiful words fill my head.

## Frivolously

Thee instruere me every night
With thy words
I studiously adhere though trucidant
Turning thy sheets carefully
I find meself soli and fidus
And no longer as vana
As whence we first met
Now thee bolsters me inner thoughts
Tempori I will benefite
Turbulentam tymes
Finds me nauseare
Fundementa I must haf
Nugatorie nos jacturea copia
Eve though copium est magnus
To be wise is to be strong!

## Lotion

Smells refreshing
Coy and clinging
Briskly rubbing
Slipree sliding
Up, down, around
Squirting flowing
Funny designs
Finally gone
It disappears

# Temple

Ornate heavy solid chestnut front door
Class inlaid brass fittings inviting more
Window panes gold mouldings designs of light
Symbols on the white brick column façade
Quiet dignity compartmentalized
Surrounding flowers a heavenly sight
Garden encompassed the tall green pines
The scenery, the building all entwines
Moroni's golden horn blows from atop
The white column jutting from the center
Complete package represents a special tone
Worthy spirits from entering don't stop

# 89

Eighty nine not ninety
One times one short
Close to one hundred
Cheyenne's fort

## Relevance

Relevance, significance, poems what?
Not many care, those that do; care a lot
Is it enough to study, justify
Poets telling themselves it's not a lie
Believing strongly albeit stulte
Words, like subtle waves, on paper does lay
Seldom escaping, minds overpower
Stopped from freedom by intell's tower
Oft not climbed tho often attempted
Brag, boast, bravado verses are tempted.


## Thoughts

I thought I was old
Until I saw Him
I thought I was bold
Until I met her.

## Poet or Not

My wife told me just the other day
Do not under any circumstances
Become a poet, cause there is no pay
No matter how many given chances
Majority of people will not read
Though spoken kindly, my heart did feel lances
A pierce to the soul, my wounded did bleed
Like horsesteps on brain matter now prances
Ballerina mincing, stepping lightly
Was my poem, beheld word dances
That's my beholden, shining not brightly
According to her (though only glances)
Poems are words of our personal life
Other lives most ideally enhances
Alleviating balm for those in strife
Only for those who are not in trances.

## Wackos

How simple life is
You hugger of tree
Strong wood leafy green
As life is simply

Save the shaded glen
A protest of man
On the wooded trail
Mankind you would ban

## Soccer

Soccer defines everyone
Enjoying sporting contests
Wildly cheering sidelines
Coaches trumpeting orders
Players listening raptly
Spherical spinning downfield
Leafy growing underneath
Grandular sweating bodies
Yellow referees blowing
Defenders offense stopping
Offense attacking always
Superstars scoring GOALSSSSS.

## The Kiss

Round red balls
Hung in halls
Green leaf bed
This way led
Set for kiss
Smooth bright lips
Head tilts up
Eyes now shut
Waits for more
By the door
Lips now brush
Heart does hush

## Gangrene

Feet rubbed
Sores forming
Wounds gaping
Red soreness
Drugs galore
Starts anew
Grows bigger
No fading
Kills owner.

## Black Jacket

The black
jacket
On him
covers
His pain
inside
It rubs
Rawhide

## Traveling

Lately man was transitorious
After visiting Egypt, I guess
Looking forward, glancing back
Seeing future is a knack
Filled with sordes thinking
Into the abyss sinking
Now seeks a true vigilare
Mankind takes a first step dare
Like leaving a foreign land
From our shoes we kick the sand.


## Not Waiting

Comatose, he rose from death's bed
Looking, acting out of his head
Seeking, finding his recompense
Dying, for him just made no sense
Standing, walking far from the grave
Loving, wishing her love to save.

# Fine

When they are fine
They are so fine
But then sometimes
They are like limes
Smooth but so sour
Green with power
Left aftertaste
Never would waste
They are so mean
Refreshing clean
Hair down or up
Tea in their cup
Even if not
Truth will be taught
So they all say
Disagree, pay
Love them and now
You take the vow
It is their hold
You can't be bold
Theirs forever
Can't leave, never
With them you're stuck
Shit out of luck!

## Signs

We see war and some cry out "lo"
Blows us all to hell
Flies planes into towers
Stirs the powers
To retaliate
Before its too late
This picture is hell
Sum, supero
I do not look
And then astonished
I ignore the signs
And await Jove.

## Life

Spring flowers
Blooming
Bright colors
Fading
Vase somber
Cracking
Green water
Flowing

## Trickles

Self-expression, from a person
Not normally speaking
From the heart
From the brain
Allows the seepage
Into false air
Wondering
Where will it go
Who will hear, feel
Or gather it in
As apples from the orchard
Or better yet
Trickles of water
From the aquaduct
To use at needy times
Just like the words and rhymes
Written by the monks
On scrolls.

## Jala

Long for its size
With a stem short
Oily look, feel
Causes retort
Curved slices
Favorite spices
Makes a meal
The real deal!

## Eden

The devil swells
With argument
Spouting words of fire
From hell sent
Convinced of his right
After the Fall
To tempt mankind
One and all
With countenance
Brightly aflame
Apples specious arguments
Mankind's great shame!

## Cantertales

Poor, poor Geoffrey
Longing to be free
From thoughts and words
Dragons and swords
Women and noble deeds
Knights and their steeds
Pilgrims telling tales
Each by other pales
Finally they are done
A tribute to his setting sun.

## Puzzle

Mighty under sedentary life in makeshift signs
And reading errors
Waiting and inviting time in nascent grimes
To omit taking annual loves
Can others not try realizing our lovers
Are not discedo
Wishful intimacy, loving levers
Denies our
Amounted not, yet time hinges in newer gains
Troubled omnipotence
Gravest elsewhere trains
In time!

# Family Death

Here I lay on this hospice bed
Family round wishing me dead
Tears in their eyes I guess of some
Even the bros who thought me dumb
A life of repose they do say
They never saw me out cutting hay
Words, he knew, rhymes, couplets and such
We knew he'd never 'mount to much
All he did the last twenty years
Pen prose filled with hope and good cheers
Look at him now all bundled up
Ready to drink from Jesus cup
Wonder what (nothing) he left to me
Probably a poem,,,,,,,tee hee
It might be worth something says one
When this life is all said and done.

## Paradise

Reprobate demons, their teeth grey gnashing
Lying in hell, hot, after their bashing
Searing, burning, scorching new memories
Brimming fiery lake, turbulent seas
Volcanic red ash stifling their throats
Dark monsters, angels, dragons and black groats
Tumultuous noise, crying, sobs and fears
Defiance, maddening thoughts through their tears
Haw many angels will rise from the dark
Their rights, their heaven, hell loudly they bark
Following a leader same as day one
Building Chaos and Pandemonium
Reveling in mankind's utter despair
Changing, modeling God's plan, do they dare?

## Night

Lovers lightly leaping
Keepers quietly creeping
Mothers models molting
Fliers frantic folding
Snores sleepy sounding.

# Funeral

Rain wet pitter-patter dripping from eaves
Silently, quietly watering sheaves
Washing away fears, as widow grieves
Mourning her loss that was stolen by thieves.

Lifting her head, as she wipes her red eyes
Red-rimmed, tear-filled from all her cries
Rising with shudders, calmness she tries
Seeing the crowd, the water now dries.

Tremulous, faltering wan her smile
Strength leading comforting her this trial
Stomach truthfully rumbling with bile
Memories crowding, set back the dial.

The day is done the shadows causing night
As one her loneliness besets with fright
Her conscious desires no longer bright
Happiness twinkles far out of sight.

## Oceanview

Blue, dark green, gray
Waves and skies
Dotted with white
Clouds and breaks
One lone seagull
On wing

## I miss her!

Do I miss her? Her smile,
Her voice, her touch, her eyes
Her understanding, her thoughts,
Her concerns voiced, her hands, her
Throat, her laugh, her eyebrows, her toes
Her feet, her eyelashes, her legs, her nose
Her compassion, her feelings.
Yes, I miss her.

## Grey Skies

The grey skies are endless
So they seem to me
Blushing with nature
Enveloping ground and tree
Not a cloud in site
Cause it's all one cloud
No hint of sunlight
But day has begun
Now I see it carries on
Forever.

## Michaelangelo

Angels, devils
Intertwined
Grasping hands
Dragging, encircling
pushing pulling
Up and down.


## Maternal Tranquility

When I see in my mind's eye
Mother's hand sprayed with flour
And smell the remembered smells
Gives me a sense of power

Only power not today
But one instilled from the past
Gives me a sense of my life
Traditions that always last.

## A&E

Fruit tree with snake
Eve bite did take
Realizing now
Broken the vow
Adam follows
His bite swallows
It had to be
Now they could see
Evil and good
Choices they could
Make wrong or right
Hide from God's sight
They are found out
Fearful, guilt, doubt
Leaving Eden
New world live in
Learn their true path
In hardship bath
To Him return
Or ever burn.

## Changes

Society used to have a role
Men learn skills, set work to
Earn the daily bread is
Their job, what they do
Come home, have dinner
Comforted by home and hearth
Content, is breadwinner
While woman at home
With abode to clean
Children to dress and comfort
Problems and solutions seen
Handled with skill, aplomb
Punishment by the dean
When he returns from day
Now society does say
Women, men are the same way
Against troubles both they flay
Which is better, worse?
Wither way is a curse.
Or blessing.

## Vicki's Sonnet

I never said the words "I do"
To another girl, not my wife
Yet lady has always been there
Knowing she would listen always
Through times of trouble I did know
We'd share kids, events and spouses
Our lives intertwined with our love
Destiny given from above
Our flames of love never douses
For each other, our blended glow
Sharing friendship for all our days
Never questioned if I do care
She's another love of my life
Our shared love forever true.

# Shrink

Yes, he says to me
I'm sure that I see
Your ideas to count
More than ones I spout
Take control I say
On the couch today
Rise up, give me hope
Wonder, can I cope
He asks looking up
Sips drink from the cup
I once for him filled
Before mind untilled
Ere hour just begun
Struggles lost and won
To me he does speak
Same time every week
Overpaid mapper
Fleeting mind's trapper
Minders of mislaid
Thoughts, no longer played
Backward or forwards
Pushes sane man towards
Insanity.

## Just you?

Self-determining masses
Broken down in classes
Surging ever onward
Pushed by the largest group
Out of life's circling loop
As individuals one
Their journey just begun
Be thee part, or just you?

## Jazz

Jazz lilting on the air
Listening people, rapt
Faces, eyes alight glow
With fire, desire, longing
Beating inside raging
With the mellowing sound
The incessant throbbing
Brings together apart
Those who are, do not wish
To be but listening
Hearing, absorbing found
Peace, tranquility share
On music stream bobbing
With life's hardening blow
No longer feeling trapt
As a stream with no fish.

## Light

Three light bulbs burning
Brightly as if yearning
For escape from incandescent
Heat and no fingers touch
Except when darkness falls.

## Moths

Is it me that invites or attracts
To my circle, like moths slipping
Closer and closer to a flame
The spurt of energy singeing
Wings, seconds of flutters
Then off to the gathering
Darkness, or drops to the floor
To lie on the cold wood beating
With breaths or beats
Of moth hearts slowing
Breath it sends flying
Back to the light circle.

## Copies

We all look the same, from behind
Says she as she walked through the room
I thought you were them, not you
It's hard to imagine that they are carbon
Copies of you.  I had nothing to do with it
She laughs, but she actually gave them
The best thing of all, not my looks or
My brains (or arrogance) but her compassion
Cause it's a proven fact that I'm not the
Empathetic one, and it's for daggone sure
That I do not feel sorry for many.

## Eyes

Bright eyes,
Honest eyes
Wise eyes
Naïve eyes
Happy eyes
Child's eyes

*J. Trapp*

## Eyes of a Child

So bright, alive
Shiny with laughs
Filling their faces
With more than joy
Creating love
Spirits above
Both girl and boy
Gathering all
To shine throughout
Spirit shows out
From deep within
They're free from sin
Shows in their eyes
Children so wise.

# Poem's New Design

The trees are blowing in the breezes
No cloud shrieking out so loud
Sky releases snow that freezes
New crowd bursting out so proud
Flowers peeking for sunshine seeking
While bugs scurry through grassy rugs
Gutters leaking like burglars sneaking
Spring hugs that enhance like drugs
We know that it is an early show
Winter fake as we all rake
Grounds flow with a winter glow
Our take as we inside bake
That spring will soon bring
Sharp fife pipes out so rife
We sing as the bells ring
New life to end our strife

## My Sonnet

I love to write in my own style
A dove so white brightens my smile
With slap of wing soars to the skies
A cap of spring words from pen flies
To know I say and some shall read
A snow of ray young mind will feed
With hope for life to testify
To cope with strife ode to the try
Now shine and glow new poem write
All mine will flow nothing too trite
I leave out nil to you goodbye
Conceive a will no asking why

A poem for you is all it took
As lying in bed your body shook.